CO-OPS, TEAMS & MMOs

By
Kirsty Holmes

CRABTREE
PUBLISHING COMPANY
WWW.CRABTREEBOOKS.COM

CRABTREE
PUBLISHING COMPANY
WWW.CRABTREEBOOKS.COM

**Published
in Canada
Crabtree Publishing**
616 Welland Avenue
St. Catharines, ON
L2M 5V6

**Published in
the United States
Crabtree Publishing**
PMB 59051
350 Fifth Ave, 59th Floor
New York, NY 10118

Published in 2019 by Crabtree Publishing Company

Author: Kirsty Holmes

Editors: Holly Duhig, Petrice Custance

Design: Gareth Liddington

Proofreader: Melissa Boyce

**Production coordinator and
 prepress technician:** Margaret Amy Salter

Print coordinator: Katherine Berti

Photo credits:
All images are courtesy of Shutterstock.com.

7 – T–Kot, Santi0103, 8 – Randy Miramontez, Kevin Chang for Team Liquid, 9 – vladibulgakov, MostlyCoffee, 10 – Blan–k, Gorodenkoff, 11 – Trifonenkolvan, 18 – Roman–Kos, OHishiapply, 22 – Benedek Alpar, 23 – Banjamin. nagel, Images are courtesy of Shutterstock.com. With thanks to Getty Images, Thinkstock Photo and iStockphoto.

World of Warcraft and Overwatch: all images courtesy of Blizzard Entertainment, Inc. All rights reserved. With grateful thanks.

Sea of Thieves: all images courtesy of Microsoft Studios and Rare, all rights reserved. With grateful thanks.

Printed in the U.S.A./012019/CG20181123

Library and Archives Canada Cataloguing in Publication

Holmes, Kirsty, author
      Co-ops, teams, and MMOs / Kirsty Holmes.

(Game on!)
Includes index.
Issued in print and electronic formats.
ISBN 978-0-7787-5258-5 (hardcover).--
ISBN 978-0-7787-5271-4 (softcover).--
ISBN 978-1-4271-2187-5 (HTML)

      1. Internet games--Juvenile literature. 2. Fantasy games--
Juvenile literature. 3. Role playing--Juvenile literature. I. Title.

GV1469.15.H64 2019   j794.8'14678   C2018-906125-1
                                               C2018-906126-X

Library of Congress Cataloging-in-Publication Data

Names: Holmes, Kirsty, author.
Title: Co-ops, teams, and MMOs / Kirsty Holmes.
Description: New York, New York : Crabtree Publishing Company, 2019. |
Series: Game on! | Includes index.
Identifiers: LCCN 2018053425 (print) | LCCN 2018056021 (ebook) |
   ISBN 9781427121875 (Electronic) |
   ISBN 9780778752585 (hardcover : alk. paper) |
   ISBN 9780778752714 (pbk. : alk. paper)
Subjects: LCSH: Internet games--Juvenile literature. | Video games--
   Juvenile literature.
Classification: LCC GV1469.15 (ebook) | LCC GV1469.15 .H64 2019 (print)
   | DDC 794.8--dc23
LC record available at https://lccn.loc.gov/2018053425

CONTENTS

WELCOME TO THE ARCADE

Do you love the thrill of the chase? Can you imagine the crowd cheering as you **electronically** score the winning goal? This guide will help you build your gaming skills and reach the top of the podium in the world of multiplayer video games. So what are you waiting for? Let's get your game on!

Hi! You must be our new teammate. We've got an hour to practice here in the Arcade before the tournament begins. I'm the team captain. Come on, let's go!

Let's start at the beginning. A video game is an electronic game that needs a player (that's you) to use a device (that's the thing you play on) to make stuff happen on a screen. Usually, that screen is a television or a personal computer (PC), but you can play games on smartphones, handheld gaming devices, and tablets. To play on your television you will need a **console**. There are lots of types of video games. From platformers and puzzlers to amazing action-adventure games, there is an exciting amount of choice in the world of gaming!

Okay, team. I want fingers on **shoulder buttons**, and thumbs and **reflexes** at the ready. The harder we work in this training session, the better our chances of winning the tournament. Let's begin!

<<Player One... Ready...?>>

DATA FILE: ONLINE AND MULTIPLAYER GAMES

Okay, Arcade, we're ready to start. Load data.

<<LOADING... DATA LEVEL ONE: WHAT IS A MULTIPLAYER GAME?>>

While lots of games can be enjoyed alone, many competitive games let people play with or against other people online. Multiplayer games allow more than one player to play in the same game at the same time. Cooperative games, or co-ops, are multiplayer games that allow players to play together as teammates toward a common goal. Massively multiplayer online games, or MMOs or MMOGs, allow large numbers of people to play against each other. Thanks to **4G**, the ability to play these games has never been better. Players can challenge each other from their smartphones while they sit on the bus on the way to school! Whether you like playing word and puzzle games or sports games, it's never been easier to play with people from around the world.

64:27 USA 2 - CAN 2

PLAYER INDICATOR

GAME INFORMATION

TEAMMATE

OPPONENT

PLAYER INFORMATION

9 Team Captain

FIELD MAP

ESPORTS

In electronic sports games, the very best players compete for the biggest prizes. The most popular games attract huge audiences, and the pros can do some incredible things with a controller or mouse.

SPORTS GAMES

Sports games are **simulations** that often include real uniforms, players, and stadiums. FIFA is probably the most famous, but most popular sports are turned into video games.

SHOOTERS

Games such as Overwatch and Fortnite place players in a **battle royale** armed to the teeth with crazy weapons and spectacular superpowers.

MMORPGS

Massively multiplayer online role-playing games allow many players to interact as characters in the game. Games such as World of Warcraft offer whole worlds to explore.

FREE-TO-PLAY

Titles such as World of Tanks are free to download, although players can also buy **unique** units, power boosters to help them in the game, and decorative items to make them stand out.

PERSISTENT WORLDS

Some games never sleep. With huge armies fighting in PlanetSide 2, and strategy battles in mobile games such as Clash of Clans, the front lines are always moving.

<<DID YOU KNOW?>>
IT IS ESTIMATED THAT THE POPULAR BATTLE ROYALE GAME FORTNITE MADE $1.5 MILLION IN ITS FIRST THREE DAYS ONLINE!

BLIZZCON

A gaming convention, or con, is a huge event in any gamer's social calendar. Conventions are large gatherings of people who all share an interest, whether it be a specific game, a brand such as Nintendo, or just video games in general. The conventions typically last two or three days. Those who attend often dress up as their favorite characters, buy merchandise, and sometimes get to meet the stars of their favorite games in person!

WORLD OF WARCRAFT

STARCRAFT II

DIABLO

HEARTHSTONE

For MMO fans, BlizzCon is the most important gaming convention of them all. Blizzard, the company that makes games such as World of Warcraft, StarCraft, and Overwatch, holds the convention every year in Anaheim, California. Fans of Blizzard games are treated to two days of game news, previews of new games, costume contests, and hands-on play with games such as Diablo, Heroes of the Storm, and Hearthstone. The convention closes with a concert, and fans are treated to a goodie bag of treats, games, and more.

COSPLAY

What do you get when you blend costumes and play? Cosplay, of course! Cosplay is a performance art where people dress up as characters from their favorite games, movies, books, or TV shows. People often spend months making their costumes, paying attention to even the tiniest detail. Cosplayers use skills such as mask-making, sculpting, makeup, wig-making, and sewing to create their amazing costumes.

In cosplay, anyone can be anything. Cosplayers don't have to stick to their own gender or age, and they can even mix up characters from different worlds or themes. When in costume, many cosplayers behave as the character, speaking and moving just as they do. At BlizzCon, there is even a competition that cosplayers can enter. There are also contests for the creation of artwork, live performances, and music inspired by the games.

TECH TALK

If you're going to get ahead in the competitive world of online gaming, you need to know what you're talking about. This data file will provide the knowledge you need to get started. Okay, Arcade, we're ready to begin.

<<LOADING... DATA LEVEL THREE: WHAT YOU NEED TO KNOW>>

TAKE AIM

A lot of online games involve having good aim. Whether you're firing paint in Splatoon, ammunition in World of Tanks, or magic spells in World of Warcraft, a big part of the action is going to involve beating an opponent. You'll need to be calm and focused to emerge victorious, and also well rested. Take regular breaks when playing and you'll stay sharp.

LEARN THE LINGO

The communities that build up around online games often start to create their own languages and phrases. For example, GG stands for "good game," something that players say to each other if they've enjoyed the match. Learn the language and talk the talk, but remember to be respectful to your fellow players.

KNOW YOUR MODE

Multiplayer games come in all shapes and sizes, but within each game there are often different ways to play. These are called modes, and each one comes with different rules and settings. It's always super important to know what is going on in each mode and how the rules differ.

PLAY THE OBJECTIVE

This might sound like common sense, but you must always remember to play the **objective**. Far too often, people get distracted or forget what they're doing, and in a close match it can make all the difference. Don't be dragged out of position and don't chase after personal glory. Work as a team and work the objective.

DOMINATE THE MAP

In a lot of multiplayer games, the action takes place on different maps, and these maps are usually quite varied in terms of how they look. More importantly, each map has features that are advantageous to the team that occupies it, whether that be a high point that lets you see more of the area around it, or a good hiding spot.

FACT FILE:

Blizzard's World of Warcraft—or WoW as it's often called—is one of the most famous games in the world. At the peak of its powers, it had millions of players logging in every day and going on fantastical adventures together with their friends. WoW is an MMORPG, which stands for massively multiplayer online role-playing game. That's a bit of a mouthful, but it basically means that it's a role-playing game that people play online together in groups.

Role-playing games usually let people create their own characters, often making them up from scratch. In WoW, players can be humans, orcs, elves, Pandarens, and more. There's a huge range of options players can use to customize their characters, something which lets people add interesting features to their made-up heroes to make them look unique and special. Once you get playing, the things you do earn points, which you can spend on **gearing up**.

Then comes the MMO part. With your special one-of-a-kind character, you head off in search of adventure, teaming up with other players to explore dungeons and hunt for loot, or battle against challenging enemy bosses. One of the best things about WoW is that it also can allow people to hang out—a big part of the experience is just hanging out with your friends.

Warcraft didn't start off as an MMORPG. Before Blizzard made this **third-person** role-playing game, it was a strategy series where players built settlements and controlled small armies. Since the success of WoW there's even been a big-budget Hollywood movie. The fantasy world remains as popular as ever.

GET YOUR GAME ON

Remember, there is no "i" in team. Every player needs to make sure they practice, practice, practice, so their skills are sharp and they are always ready to compete. Let's look at some of the things we'll need to remember.

<<LOADING... DATA LEVEL FOUR: THINGS YOU'LL NEED TO KEEP IN MIND>>

BUILD YOURSELF

Some games offer a level playing field, where every player goes into battle with the same gear and it's all about skill. Other games, however, allow you to build your character or team over time. Spend time making sure you've upgraded your **loadout** so you're at full strength when you go up against human opponents.

TECH PRACTICE

Before you take on other players, why not test yourself against the computer? Some online games come with **tutorials** which show you the ropes. Other games have short single-player **campaigns** which might take four or five hours to complete but give you a small taste of everything the game has to offer.

TAKE IT SLOW

Slow and steady is always best, especially when you're new to a game. Rushing into the action can often result in an untimely end, so it's always a good idea to put the brakes on before you **engage** the enemy and assess the situation. If you're outnumbered and outgunned, it might be better to avoid a particular fight.

WEAPONIZE

Every weapon (or player, if you're playing a sports game) has a **specialty**, and using it effectively and also at the right time is the key to success. For example, there's no point firing a sniper rifle up close, and using your goalkeeper up front means you won't score many goals.

MAKE FRIENDS

With a friend by your side, your chances of winning are doubled, and if you and your opponent are evenly matched, your teammate will make all the difference. Always pay attention to what your friends are doing, talk over a microphone if you have one, and stick closely together in the game whenever you have the chance.

TIME YOUR MOVE

Whether you're waiting for a certain weapon to **spawn** on the map, or for a character's special ability to come online, part of successful play is timing your attack and making sure you're at your strongest when your enemy is at their weakest.

FACT FILE: EA SPORTS

EA Sports has developed a reputation over the years for making some of the very best sports games. The studio aims to create realistic experiences, or simulations, of different sports, including soccer, hockey, and basketball. These games include a number of different ways to play, either alone, with people at home, or online against your friends. Let's take a look at the different ways you can play sports games.

The EA Sports FIFA video game series is probably the most popular sports video game in the world. With so many fans, it offers a whole range of ways to play. You can't always keep everyone happy, but EA certainly tries. For example, if you want to live the life of a real player, you can take control of a young player and follow his career, taking part in games and controlling the action as you try to score important goals for the team. If you prefer a bit more control, you can become the manager of an entire team, making every decision from which players to sign to how much they get paid. When you're not managing, you also play the games, controlling the whole team in every match throughout a whole season.

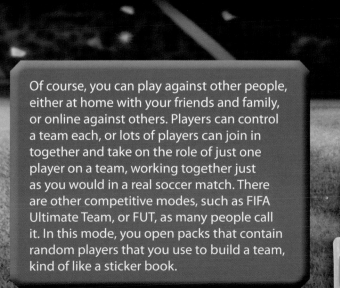

Of course, you can play against other people, either at home with your friends and family, or online against others. Players can control a team each, or lots of players can join in together and take on the role of just one player on a team, working together just as you would in a real soccer match. There are other competitive modes, such as FIFA Ultimate Team, or FUT, as many people call it. In this mode, you open packs that contain random players that you use to build a team, kind of like a sticker book.

XBOX 360 — **FIFA 15**

XBOX 360 — **FIFA 14**

XBOX 360 — **FIFA 13**

XBOX 360 — **FIFA 12**

XBOX 360 — **FIFA 11**

XBOX 360 — **FIFA 10**

XBOX 360 — FIFA 09

XBOX 360 — FIFA 08

XBOX 360 — FIFA 07

XBOX — FIFA 06

XBOX — FIFA Football 2005

XBOX — FIFA Football 2004

XBOX — FIFA FOOTBALL 2003

ESPORTS

People have been playing games since the beginning of time, and people have been competing with each other and enjoying friendly competition for just as long. So it was only a matter of time for sports competitions to enter the digital world. In just a few short years, esports has grown into a multi-billion-dollar industry, with professional players, coaches, and teams competing in leagues and tournaments. Matches play out in packed stadiums, and the best players can earn huge amounts of money.

Esports games come in all shapes and sizes, from competitive card games such as Hearthstone: Heroes of Warcraft to colorful shooters such as Fortnite. Among the most popular games in the world of esports are MOBAs, or multiplayer online battle arenas, where players control a character as part of a small team and then attack another team until one side has overpowered the other. DOTA 2 and League of Legends are by far the biggest games of this type.

Cartoon-style competitive shooters such as Overwatch and Splatoon 2 also attract plenty of interest, and exist alongside military titles such as Call of Duty and Counter-Strike. The shooter game Fortnite, which started out as a base-building co-op game, soon shot to superstardom thanks to its colorful and light-hearted approach to the battle royale formula that has every player fending for themselves. It doesn't hurt that it's a free-to-play game, so that anyone who owns a console can get involved.

Esports is big business and the competitions building around the most popular games are drawing in huge crowds. Media outlets cover these competitions alongside regular sports, **sponsors** pay players and teams, and the best players are becoming celebrities in their own right with adoring fans and big prizes up for grabs.

FACT FILE: Sea of Thieves

Sea of Thieves is a co-op game that sends comical pirates off on the trail of adventure, where crews of up to four players can team up and go in search of buried treasure. What makes Sea of Thieves such a magical experience is the cooperation that it requires from teammates. You don't just point your ship at an island and head off into the sunset, you have to roll down the sails and face them into the wind, build up speed, and avoid dangerous rocks that strike out of the water in hopes of catching sailors unaware.

Half of the fun in Sea of Thieves is playing with your friends as you take on skeleton pirates and follow treasure maps—and remember, X always marks the spot! The huge open sea contains lots of islands full of hidden secrets, and as you sail, there are shipwrecks to explore, angry storms to avoid, and even the odd sea monster waiting to wrap its giant tentacles around your ship and pull you down into the depths of the ocean.

Things get really interesting when you meet up with another crew of pirates. Some sail smaller, quick-moving ships, while other crews will control giant ships armed with many cannons. Sometimes these ships will pass each other without any trouble, but other times there can be huge battles that sometimes last for ages, with cannonballs flying through the air while sharks swim patiently under the water, waiting for anyone foolish enough to dive in.

Sea of Thieves is what you might call a sandbox game, which means it's a huge world where you make your own fun using the tools and activities given to you. The focus here isn't on playing through a big story, instead it's up to the players to make their own fun.

CONSOLE PROFILE

Microsoft has released three different Xbox consoles over the years, but could the latest mean the end of the old console generation cycle?

2001: XBOX

The first Xbox console launched in 2001. Before that, Microsoft was best known for making operating systems and software. The console launched in the U.S. first, then in Europe the following year. It was Microsoft's first move into the console space and the first time we saw the company's hugely popular title, Halo.

2002: XBOX LIVE

Microsoft launched Xbox Live in 2002. This online service brought players together for friendly online competition, but it was the launch of Halo 2 that really put Live on the map. For many console players, it marked the first time they were able to play against other people from the comfort of their sofa.

XBOX

2017: XBOX ONE X

The Xbox brand looked to be in trouble, but after much thought and research, the company came back strong with the most powerful console the world has ever seen, the Xbox One X. The company also outlined its intentions to do away with the old console cycle, making many original Xbox and 360 titles compatible with the Xbox One, and suggesting a future where players will be able to take their libraries of games to all future consoles. They even opened up the platform to the PC space, with all games now launching on Windows 10 PCs.

2005: XBOX 360

The Xbox 360 put Microsoft ahead in the console wars, thanks in part to the move online, but also because of the exclusive games that appeared on the console. Halo returned, Gears of War and Forza both got started, and for a time, Microsoft's console was the best console to own.

360 CONTROLLER

Microsoft didn't get the first Xbox controller quite right, it was too big to use comfortably, but the one that came with the Xbox 360 was a hit. Not only was it an excellent controller, it was also PC-compatible, helping it become the standard controller for PC gamers too.

2013: XBOX ONE

When Microsoft announced the Xbox One, some of the plans for the console were very unpopular, such as needing the Kinect to be plugged in at all times, which raised privacy concerns. Several features had to be scrapped before the console launched in late 2013.

2010: KINECT

Kinect was a camera system that started on the 360 and ended on the Xbox One. The Kinect turned the player's body into the controller, although it wasn't always smooth sailing and some games didn't quite deliver the experience the developers clearly wanted. The Kinect returned, bundled in with every Xbox One at launch, but the tech didn't catch on and in the end Microsoft had to ditch it.

HORIZON

FACT FILE: MOBAS

Some of the most popular competitive games are multiplayer online battle arenas, or MOBAs. These games developed from a **mod** made to an old strategy game called Warcraft III: Reign of Chaos, which first landed in 2002. Modders adapted the real-time strategy game and gave it new rules, rules that are basically the same today. Players, controlling powerful hero characters, must battle each other, computer-controlled minions, and turrets located across three lanes, and work their way toward the enemy base to destroy a structure called the ancient. The game mode was called Defense of the Ancients, or DOTA for short.

The first actual game to be released in the MOBA style was League of Legends, or LoL for short (most games in this **genre** have shortened names based on the initial letters of each word in their title, which are called acronyms). LoL follows the DOTA template quite closely, and as a result, it is played by millions of people every day. It's also a free-to-play game, which means anyone can play, although non-paying players will have a limited number of characters to choose from. In fact, most MOBAS are free-to-play, as it's hard to compete against huge titles such as LoL if you're asking people to pay up front.

League of Legends is a hugely popular game, with professional teams competing in leagues around the world for cash prizes, but LoL can't compare to DOTA 2, another popular MOBA made by Valve (the company that runs the biggest PC gaming platform, Steam) that every year offers millions in prize money to the best teams. Those two games are monsters of the genre, but Blizzard rejoined the MOBA scene (after all, it was their game, Warcraft III, that got this whole party started in the first place) with Heroes of the Storm (bet you can figure out what that's called for short).

PRO TALK

Let's find out more about games by talking to some professionals. Gaming professionals are people who do something in gaming to earn a living, such as making video games or writing about them in magazines. These pros really know their stuff, so let's hear their advice and tips.

JACK STEWART

Jack Stewart is an esports journalist. He writes about the latest gaming news and tournament results, and interviews professional players. Let's find out more…

1. WHY DO YOU THINK PEOPLE ENJOY ESPORTS?

"You want to win and prove you're the best. Watching the best players in the world is so fun and it's great getting to support your favorite team. I sit at home and cheer on my favorite League of Legends (LoL) and Overwatch teams the same way I cheer for my favorite football team."

2. WHAT WERE YOUR FAVORITE GAMES AS A CHILD?

"I would play Pokémon nonstop for HOURS! Gold was the first one I played but Emerald will always be my favorite (Mudkip is my favorite starter). I also always picked up the new FIFA and WWE games every year. The Smackdown vs Raw series was especially great."

3. WHAT TIPS AND TRICKS CAN YOU GIVE US IF WE WANT TO GET BETTER AT GAMING?

"Other than practicing, I'd say try to predict what your opponents are going to do. If you're one or two steps ahead of your enemies, you'll be able to surprise them and have the advantage. You also may not realize it but eating healthy food and exercising will help a lot, too. You'll have more energy and your reaction times will be way faster. That's why you see a lot of esports players going to the gym!"

4. WHAT ARE THE BEST AND WORST THINGS ABOUT YOUR JOB?

"The best part of my job is I get to travel around the world and write about the gaming tournaments that I love. The downside is I now don't have as much time to play games anymore, although I still manage to squeeze a few in!"

5. WHAT ADVICE WOULD YOU GIVE A YOUNG PERSON WHO WANTS TO GET INTO GAMING PROFESSIONALLY?

"Find a game that you're good at and really enjoy playing, if you want to go pro you'll have to play that game for the next few years! If you're able to, watch replays of your own matches. Seeing your gameplay from a different perspective will help you fix a lot of mistakes. Finally, I'd say once you get to a good level, make friends with pro players online. They'll give good advice and could help you join a team."

FACT FILE: OVERWATCH

Blizzard doesn't do shooters, that's what people said. That was certainly the general opinion before Overwatch landed back in 2016. Nobody is saying that anymore.

Overwatch has been growing steadily since its launch, with millions and millions of players signing up for duty over the past couple of years in this online hero shooter. The game launched with a range of colorful characters, but the secret to Overwatch's success is that the developers have never rested, with the game being updated regularly with new hero characters to learn, different maps to play on, and surprising game modes to keep things fresh.

Each Overwatch character is unique, and fulfills a special role on the battlefield. Mercy, for example, is what you would call a **support**, and although she won't do much damage to the enemy herself, her primary role is to heal her teammates and keep them in the fight. Hanzo, on the other hand, is a DPS character, which stands for damage per second. He fires his deadly bow at enemies. Another DPS character named Tracer is able to travel through time. **Tanks** such as Winston are always on the front line, absorbing damage while they keep the opponent busy. There are well over 20 heroes to choose from, and each one has their own strengths and weaknesses.

As you play a typical game of Overwatch, players have to work together to achieve different objectives, such as protecting or attacking a certain section of the map. Teams have to coordinate, not just in the game, but in terms of the characters they choose to play as, and getting the right mix of characters is the key to success.

As the **roster** of characters increases, so does the game's popularity. In 2018, Blizzard started the Overwatch League, or OWL. The league is made up of professional teams from around the world that play Overwatch in competitions.

Learning More

Okay, guys, it's time to take our places in the competition. With all this training, we can't lose. Let's go! Or do you want a little more time before we head to the arena?

<<CONTINUE? Y/N>>
WWW.ESLGAMING.COM/

<<CONTINUE? Y/N>>
WWW.EASPORTS.COM/

<<CONTINUE? Y/N>>
WWW.SEAOFTHIEVES.COM/

<<CONTINUE? Y/N>>
HTTPS://PLAYOVERWATCH.COM/EN-US/

<<CONTINUE? Y/N>>
HTTPS://WORLDOFWARCRAFT.COM/EN-US/

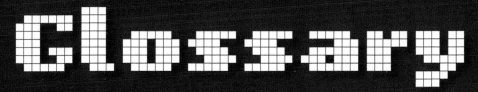Glossary

4G	The fourth generation of wireless technology that allows wireless Internet access at very high speeds
battle royale	A fight with many players that ends when only one player remains
campaign	A continuing storyline or set of adventures
console	A computer system that connects video games to a screen
electronically	Powered by electricity
engage	To take part or become involved in something
gearing up	To improve your weapons or buy better ones
genre	A particular type of something
loadout	A set of objects or weapons carried into battle
mod	Short for modification, a way to change a feature or format in a game
objective	The main goal or target
reflexes	The natural ability to react quickly
roster	A list of the name of people in a group
shoulder buttons	The buttons on the edge of the controller above the trigger
simulation	An imitation of a real-world situation
spawn	To produce or create something
specialty	A particular skill someone has gained through practice
sponsor	A person or organization who supplies money for a project
support	A type of character that is responsible for helping teammates
tank	A type of character that protects allies and occupies the front line
third person	To view the action from outside the game
tutorial	A teaching level in which gamers learn the controls for a particular game
unique	To be the only one of a particular kind

<<SAVING KNOWLEDGE. DO NOT SHUT DOWN.>>

Index

<<THANKS FOR ACCESSING THE ARCADE TODAY. WE HOPE YOU HAD THE BEST TIME. SHUTTING DOWN IN 3... 2... 1...>>